Happy Birthday, Martin Luther King

by Jean Marzollo

W9-BUS-388

Illustrated by Brian J. Pinkney

SCHOLASTIC INC.

New York Toronto London Auckland Sydney
Mexico City New Delhi Hong Kong Buenos Aires

This book was originally published in hardcover
by Scholastic Press in 1993.

ISBN-13: 978-0-439-78224-1
ISBN-10: 0-439-78224-4

30   20/0

Printed in the U.S.A.   40
First Bookshelf edition, January 2006

Designed by Adrienne M. Syphrett
The artist used scratchboard and oil pastels for his illustrations.

To Alana Jerrae Regina Prince,
born April 11, 1991, and to the memory
of Ronald Patten, 1961–1990
— J.M.

To my mother-in-law, Gwen,
and
my father-in-law, Phil
— B.P.

Foreword for Parents and Teachers

The tragic fact of Martin Luther King's murder may be too difficult and too distracting for preschoolers to deal with. If you feel that the words "shot and killed" on page 30 are inappropriate for the child or children you plan to read this book to, you may want to change the words and say simply that Martin Luther King "died" in 1968.

It isn't, after all, necessary for us to tell very young children the harsh details about Reverend King's death in order to convey to them the central message of his inspirational leadership; and perhaps that is why, when we tell young children the story of Abraham Lincoln, we usually don't tell them he was assassinated either. We seem to sense that young children can wait until they are older to learn about these terrible realities.

And yet, because Martin Luther King's murder is still fresh in our minds, we may want to tell children about his death and to include them in the process of our unfinished grief. I believe that, if we handle the subject sensitively, we will find that children, like ourselves, can look at truth and cope with death—even violent death, and that they, like us, will find through grieving that death gives meaning to life.

Jean Marzollo

Martin Luther King, Jr., was born
on January 15, 1929, in Atlanta, Georgia.
His parents loved him very much.

Martin Luther King had the same name as his father — except for one thing. His father was called Martin Luther King, Sr.; Martin was called Martin Luther King, Jr.

Martin went to elementary school, high school, and college in Atlanta. He was a good student. Later he went to divinity school in Pennsylvania.

Martin became a pastor — just like his dad — at the Ebenezer Baptist Church in Atlanta. They were both called "Reverend": the Reverend Martin Luther King, Sr., and the Reverend Martin Luther King, Jr.

Martin's job as a minister was to help people in need. He visited sick people in the hospital and made them feel better.

He asked people not to fight with each other. He said that there were peaceful ways to solve problems.

And like his father, Martin led people in prayer and song.

The Reverend Martin Luther King, Jr., is famous because he helped our country change some of its laws. A law is like a rule. Once there was a law in some places that said only white people could sit in the front of a bus and that black people had to sit in the back.

Martin Luther King said this law needed to be changed. Rosa Parks and other people helped him change it. Now all people can sit in any empty seat they like.

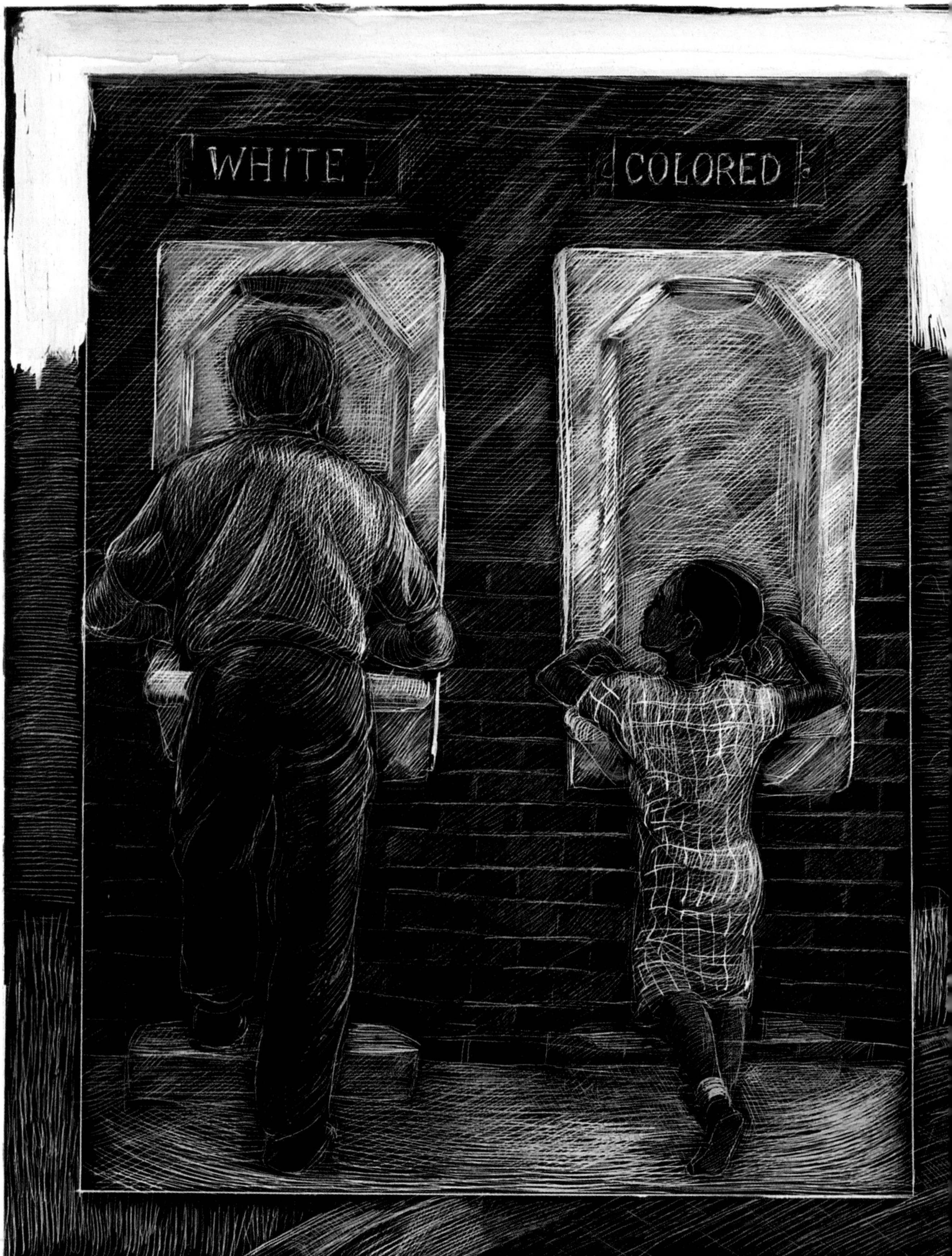
WHITE
COLORED

Once there were laws in some places that said that African-Americans could use only certain restaurants and drinking fountains. Martin Luther King and many other people helped change these laws. Now all people can share the same restaurants and drinking fountains.

Once there was a law in some places that said that black children and white children couldn't go to school together. Martin Luther King and other people, including many very brave children, had this law changed, too. Now black children and white children can go to school together.

Martin Luther King had a special talent for leadership. When he spoke, people listened. Poor people, rich people, white people, black people, and people from all around the world listened when Martin Luther King spoke. Many helped him work, march, sing, and pray for justice.

In the summer of 1963 Martin Luther King, Jr., gave the most famous speech of his life. He gave it outdoors to a quarter of a million people who had come to Washington, DC, to ask the President for jobs and freedom for black people. In his speech Martin Luther King said that he had a dream. His dream was that people everywhere would learn to live together without being mean to one another.

Martin Luther King, Jr., was shot and killed in 1968. Because he loved poor people so much, he was given a special funeral in Atlanta, Georgia, where he was born. His body was put in a simple farm cart and pulled slowly by two mules to a cemetery. Thousands of people walked behind Martin in a sad, loving parade.

On his gravestone were carved these beautiful words, "Free at last, free at last! Thank God Almighty, I'm free at last."

Martin Luther King wanted people to be able to go places together, share food together, and love one another in peace. Because he worked so hard for freedom and helped so many people gain it, we honor him every year on his special day. We call this day Martin Luther King Day, and we say to him, "Happy birthday, Martin Luther King!"